RICKY TIMS

CELTIC FANTASY

RHAPSODY QUILTS

- ■ **DESIGN COMPANION VOL. 3 TO *RICKY TIMS' RHAPSODY QUILTS***
- ■ **FULL-SIZE FREEZER PAPER PATTERN** ■ **BONUS APPLIQUÉ DESIGNS & IDEAS**

C&T PUBLISHING

Text copyright © 2008 by Ricky Tims

Artwork copyright © 2008 by C&T Publishing, Inc., and Ricky Tims

Publisher: Amy Marson

Creative Director: Gailen Runge

Acquisitions Editor: Jan Grigsby

Editor: Liz Aneloski

Technical Editors: Ellen Pahl and Helen Frost

Copyeditor/Proofreader: Wordfirm Inc.

Cover Designer: Kristen Yenche

Design Direction: Kristen Yenche and Kiera Lofgreen

Book Designer: Kerry Graham

Production Coordinator: Zinnia Heinzmann

Illustrator: Gregg Valley

Photography by Luke Mulks and Diane Pedersen of C&T Publishing, Inc., unless otherwise noted

Published by C&T Publishing, Inc., P.O. Box 1456, Lafayette, CA 94549

All rights reserved. No part of this work covered by the copyright hereon may be used in any form or reproduced by any means—graphic, electronic, or mechanical, including photocopying, recording, taping, or information storage and retrieval systems—without written permission from the publisher. The copyrights on individual artworks are retained by the artists as noted in *Celtic Fantasy—Rhapsody Quilts*. These designs may be used to make items only for personal use or donation to nonprofit groups for sale. Each piece of finished merchandise for sale must carry a conspicuous label with the following information: Designs copyright © 2008 by Ricky Tims from the book *Celtic Fantasy—Rhapsody Quilts* from C&T Publishing, Inc.

Attention Copy Shops: Please note the following exception—publisher and author give permission to photocopy pages 8, 9, and the pullout pages for personal use only.

Attention Teachers: C&T Publishing, Inc., encourages you to use this book as a text for teaching. Contact us at 800-284-1114 or www.ctpub.com for more information about the C&T Teachers' Program.

We take great care to ensure that the information included in our products is accurate and presented in good faith, but no warranty is provided nor are results guaranteed. Having no control over the choices of materials or procedures used, neither the author nor C&T Publishing, Inc., shall have any liability to any person or entity with respect to any loss or damage caused directly or indirectly by the information contained in this book. For your convenience, we post an up-to-date listing of corrections on our website (www.ctpub.com). If a correction is not already noted, please contact our customer service department at ctinfo@ctpub.com or at P.O. Box 1456, Lafayette, CA 94549.

Trademark (™) and registered trademark (®) names are used throughout this book. Rather than use the symbols with every occurrence of a trademark or registered trademark name, we are using the names only in the editorial fashion and to the benefit of the owner, with no intention of infringement.

Printed in the United States of America

10 9 8 7 6 5 4 3 2 1

CONTENTS

INTRODUCTION

Celtic designs, including knots and other interlaced motifs, have always been favorites among quilters. The intriguing interweave of these designs is both breathtaking and imaginative. In my travels to Scotland, Ireland, and North and South Wales, as well as to England, I have been privileged to witness firsthand the use of Celtic imagery in architecture, art, crafts, and textiles. There seems to be a wonderful connection to the past in these designs. Even in newer ones (such as those I have created for this book), the motifs still feel old, expressing a deep connection to the past.

The designs I created for this book were drawn from my imagination. I didn't research to find out whether there were specific rules associated with this type of design. As an artist, I desire to achieve something original even when I am influenced by something familiar. Therefore, my designs are probably best called "Celtic-ish"—meaning they are derived from my *impressions* of typical Celtic designs.

As with each supplement to *Ricky Tims' Rhapsody Quilts*, this book has a project that you can make. Remember, however, that my desire is to guide you to be original. Use any of the skeletons and appliqué designs in combination with your own or view them simply as inspiration and let your imagination soar. Whichever your path, you will undoubtedly create a quilt that is unique and beautiful.

In closing—and before you begin—let me share with you my favorite old Irish Blessing:

Deep peace of the running wave to you.

Deep peace of the flowing air to you.

Deep peace of the quiet earth to you.

Deep peace of the shining stars to you.

Moon and stars pour their healing light on you.

Deep peace to you.

Ricky Tims

A Gaelic Blessing

A Gaelic Blessing, 48″ × 48″, completed in 2008. Designed by Ricky Tims. Machine pieced, machine appliquéd, and machine quilted by Sharon Murphy.

All page references are to *Ricky Tims' Rhapsody Quilts*, unless otherwise noted.

Materials

Fabric amounts are based on 42˝-wide fabric.

Refer to Selecting Fabrics (page 35) for guidance as needed.

Fabric A: 1³⁄₈ yards

Fabric B: 3 yards

Fabric C: 1¼ yards

Fabric D: 3 yards

Assorted fabrics in coordinating colors for appliqués: 1 yard total

Binding: ½ yard

Backing: 3 yards

Batting: 52˝ × 52˝

16˝-wide fusible web: 5 yards

Thread: assorted colors to contrast with appliqué fabrics

Cutting and Preparing the Fabrics

For these steps, refer to Preparing the Master Template (page 34) and Preparing the Units (pages 38–39) for guidance as needed.

1. Use the pattern on the pullout at the back of this book to create full-size templates. You will need to trace the center template 2 times to make 2 pieces. Then tape them together to create the complete template for piece 1. Be sure to transfer all registration marks. Match the connecting lines to create complete templates for pieces 2 and 6.

2. Iron the freezer paper templates to the right side of the following fabrics. Then rough cut the fabric about ½˝ from the edge of the freezer paper.

> **From Fabric A,** cut 1 of piece 1 and 4 of piece 4.
>
> **From Fabric B,** cut 4 *each* of pieces 2 and 6.
>
> **From Fabric C,** cut 4 *each* of pieces 3 and 5.
>
> **From Fabric D,** cut 4 of piece 7.

3. Stay stitch around each template and add the registration marks in the seam allowances.

4. Trim the seam allowances to a scant ¼˝, remove the freezer paper, and place the fabric pieces on a design wall.

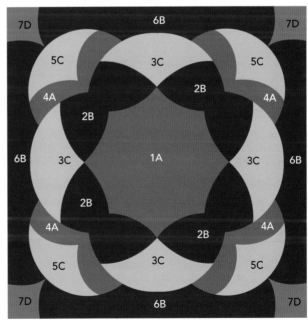

Skeleton layout—Number indicates piece number, and letter indicates fabric.

Adding the Appliqués

For these steps, refer to Machine Appliqué Techniques—Fear Not the "A" Word (pages 47–57) as needed. After cutting background pieces 1–7, use the remainder of Fabric B for the large appliqués in pieces 3 and 5. Use the remainder of Fabric D for the large central appliqué in piece 1 and for the large appliqués in pieces 2, 4, and 6. Use the assorted fabrics in coordinating colors for the flower petal and flower center appliqués in pieces 1, 2, and 3 and for the corner appliqués in piece 7.

1. Trace the appliqué designs from the pullout onto the paper side of the fusible web. (The appliqué design in piece 6 would also make a great quilting pattern.)

2. Adhere the fusible web to your chosen fabrics and prepare the appliqués. Refer to the diagram on page 7 and the photo on page 4 of this book for guidance as you fuse the appliqués onto the appropriate background pieces.

3. Use a machine single or double blanket stitch and threads that contrast in color to the various appliqué fabrics to stitch around the edges of each appliqué shape. Stitch lines over the appliqués as needed to create the over-and-under effect of a Celtic knot.

Assembling the Quilt

For this step, refer to No-Pins Precision Curved Piecing (pages 38–41), Sewing the Pieces Together (pages 57–58), Preparing Units for Set-In Curved Corners (pages 62–63), and Setting in a Curved Corner (pages 64–65) for guidance as needed.

Refer to the skeleton layout diagram on page 5 of this book. Beginning with the center (piece 1), assemble the skeleton by adding pieces in numerical order, aligning the stay stitching and registration marks and straightening the curves as you sew.

Finishing the Quilt

For these steps, refer to Tips for Quilting Your Rhapsody Quilt (page 69) for guidance as needed.

1. Mark, layer, and baste your quilt in preparation for quilting.

2. Machine quilt as desired. *A Gaelic Blessing* was quilted by outline stitching around each appliqué.

3. Trim the batting and backing even with the raw edge of the quilt top.

4. Cut 6 strips $2\frac{1}{8}'' \times 42''$ from the binding fabric. Sew the strips together end to end with diagonal seams. Use this long strip to bind the edges of the quilt.

tip

To create Celtic designs for quilting, adapt or modify some of the appliqué patterns, including those on the pattern for A Gaelic Blessing.

Skeleton with appliqués in place

ADDITIONAL DESIGNS TO TRY

Nine New Skeletons

Here are nine additional skeleton designs you can choose from to create your own Celtic Fantasy—or any other—Rhapsody quilt. Simply enlarge the pattern of your choice to the desired size, as described in Creating a Full-Size Pattern (pages 30–33), and add appliqué. On the pullout pages of this book, you'll find a variety of Celtic knot, ribbon, and vine appliqué designs that you can use as is or adapt for use with any of these skeletons.

Skeleton 3

Skeleton 1—see page 14 of this book to see this skeleton transformed into fabric with appliqué added.

Skeleton 4

Skeleton 2

Skeleton 5

Skeleton 8

Skeleton 9

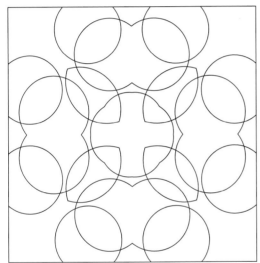

Skeleton 6

Skeleton 7

Celtic Knot, Ribbon, and Vine Appliqué Designs

The patterns on the pullout page provide a wide variety of appliqué designs featuring Celtic knots, ribbons, vines, and creatures. You can use many of these designs as is to fit the skeletons on pages 8–9 of this book. In some cases, you will need to reduce, enlarge, or customize the designs to fit your particular space. For example, you can take a basic knot design that is

long, narrow, and thin ...

... and make it short, wide, and plump.

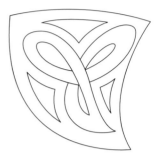

If you like, you can add filler "bits."

You can even link the motifs—a great option for borders.

Of course, you can also create your own original appliqué designs. Creating an original Celtic knot design—with its over-and-under loops—is much like working a puzzle. It is also lots of fun! Just be sure to keep an eraser nearby for modifying as you go.

Mark lightly with a pencil to fill the space with a simple line drawing.

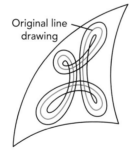

Original line drawing

"Fatten" the original drawing by marking new lines on both sides of the original.

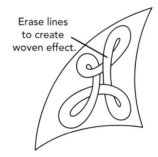

Erase lines to create woven effect.

Erase the original line drawing and the appropriate lines at the intersections to create the over-and-under effect of a Celtic knot.

You can leave the loops rounded or taper them like this.

Refer to Designing the Appliqué (pages 42–46) for more information about how to plan and adapt appliqué designs.

QUILTS FOR INSPIRATION

There is nothing like looking at a beautifully designed quilt to give you inspiration!
Here are a few examples that I hope will make your fingers itch for fabric and thread.

Cwlwm Lafant by Gwenfai Griffiths, 82″ × 82″.

"After attending Ricky's seminar in Houston, I couldn't wait to start on my own Rhapsody quilt. The quilt's name is Welsh and is inspired by a lavender knot garden. *Cwlwm Lafant* (pronounced Koo-loom Lav-ant) when translated is lavender knot. I thought the combination of the Japanese fabrics and the Rhapsody pattern would make an interesting quilt. The floral inspiration is from the Rose of Sharon block which is hand appliquéd using both freezer paper and the needle-turn method. I included a hand stitched Celtic pattern to divide the two floral areas. I added hand embroidered details (through only the top layer) and abundant hand quilting."

Twist by Elsie Vredenburg, 62˝ × 62˝.

"My first Rhapsody quilt was a result of attending Ricky's 2-day seminar. Then, I decided to make a second when Ricky began his Rhapsody reality blog on *The Quilt Show* website. The result is *Twist*. The appliqué designs were inspired by the *Great Book of* *Celtic Patterns* by Lora S. Irish, and a quilting video by Sharon Schamber was the inspiration for the tiny quilted feathers all over the quilt (much easier than large ones)."

Celtic Rhapsody by Sharon Murphy, 68″ × 68″.

"An Irish heritage, combined with a passion for weaving movement and color together in unique ways—these were the inspiration behind my *Celtic Rhapsody*. Appliqué, piecing, and trapunto techniques incorporate Ricky's hand-dyed fabrics. The star-like pattern weaves together a series of Celtic knots, leafy vines, and interconnected blocks of color, all of which encircle a Celtic Tree of Life in full flower. I utilized trapunto in the quilt's borders to create a softer echo of the leaf/vine elements. I finished the edge with piped binding."

Skeleton 1
(page 8 of this book)
without appliqué

Skeleton 1
with appliqué

Skeleton
without appliqué

Skeleton
with appliqué

ABOUT RICKY

Ricky Tims has successfully blended two diverse passions into one very unique and interesting career. His skills as a pianist, composer, and producer have been affirmed by the thousands who have heard his music. His success as a quilter is equally significant.

Ricky's innovative and entertaining presentations feature live music and humor, combined with scholarly insights and wisdom. His quilts have been displayed worldwide and are highly regarded as excellent examples of contemporary quilts with traditional appeal. Ricky Tims and Alex Anderson co-host a program called *The Quilt Show* (www.thequiltshow.com), a worldwide video/web magazine and online community for quilters that has become an Internet sensation.

He began designing and making quilts in 1991. In 2002, he was selected as one of the Thirty Most Distinguished Quilters in the World. He maintains an international schedule of teaching and speaking engagements, presents *Ricky Tims' Super Quilt Seminars* in select cities throughout the United States, and holds weeklong retreats in La Veta, a tiny mountain town in south central Colorado. He and life partner, Justin Shults, own Tims Art Quilt Studio and Gallery, a space dedicated to promoting quilting as art.

Ricky began formal music lessons at the age of three. He is a pianist, conductor, composer, arranger, music producer, and performing artist. Tims' music is neither classical, new age, pop, nor world, and yet it could fall under any of those classifications.

Sacred Age, his newest recording, was released in January 2006. The album project, featuring solo piano infused with Native American instruments, string orchestra, and vocal orchestrations, was created to suggest the beauty, majesty, and spirit of the Spanish Peaks region of southern Colorado. Tims' music has wide appeal for a diverse audience and has been described as "George Winston meets Carlos Nakai meets Yanni."

Visit Ricky's website at www.rickytims.com.

For a list of other fine books from C&T Publishing, ask for a free catalog:

C&T Publishing, Inc.
P.O. Box 1456
Lafayette, CA 94549

(800) 284-1114
Email: ctinfo@ctpub.com
Website: www.ctpub.com

C&T Publishing's professional photography services are now available to the public. Visit us at www.ctmediaservices.com.

For quilting supplies:

Cotton Patch
1025 Brown Ave.
Lafayette, CA 94549

(800) 835-4418 or
(925) 283-7883
Email: CottonPa@aol.com
Website: www.quiltusa.com